AF327174

Copyright 2013 by Felipe Benítez Reyes
Translation copyright 2013 by Emily Toder

Originally published in Spanish as
Los astrólogos errantes (Ediciones Espuela de Plata, 2005)

First Edition, First Printing
Ugly Duckling Presse
232 3rd Street, #E303, Brooklyn, NY 11215
uglyducklingpresse.org

Artwork by Julia Goldberg
Collage (page 4) by the author
Design by Don't Look Now!
Typeset in Avenir and Jenson

Printed on recycled paper and bound
at McNaughton & Gunn in Saline, Michigan
in a limited edition of 700 copies

ISBN 978-1-937027-34-6
Distributed to the trade by SPD / Small Press Distribution
www.spdbook.org

Felipe Benítez Reyes

The Errant Astrologers

translated from the Spanish by Emily Toder

Ugly Duckling Presse

The Errant Astrologers

a legend in verse in three acts

Act One

Three astrologer monarchs, in kingdoms far apart, dreamed the same dream one night. In the dream appeared a never-seen and radiant star that looked like a nomadic jewel as it suddenly faded, plunging into emptiness like those suicidal stars we call fleeting, and leaving in its wake a shimmering trail, though it shone again elsewhere, like a lit-up toy, errant in the blackness of light.

Upon rising, each king interpreted that common dream differently, though all three understood that the dreamed-of star was the sign of a real star, because stars never shine in vain, not even in the dreams of idle kings.

So those monarchs, in their remote kingdoms, spent years and years watching over the firmament by night, until they knew the palpitations of each celestial body more exactly than those of their own hearts.

Some stewards attributed that vigil to the particular eccentricities of those born into power. Others lamented the sleepless insanity that afflicted their lords, obsessed before the theater over which the moon presides.

Others, those with dark souls, conspired against their king.

Years and years passed.

Years and more years passed.

Until one night a single star imprinted its shine in the sky and all three kings knew at once that it was the star from the dream, and all three understood that they had to follow it.

The story that follows is the story of that journey.

And it is also the story of all stars that appear in dreams.

[desert night, full moon]

amerín

The blind night,
and the moon that is the eye of the blind night,
the eye that looks at me
with the white look of the blind,
because the night is blind,
and the moon is the blind eye that looks at me
and sees me not.
I wander blinded by the blind night.
I float in the darkness
as the moon floats,
the blind eye,
and the blind night,
and the blind moon as well,
the useless eye,
and I wander blind,
invisible in this great dimness of blind theater.
What am I doing here?
What are you doing there? you ask.
What are you doing there,
directionless in the blind night,
pilgrim of what,
spy of the dark without a cause,
prowling about?
The answer is simple: I have a path.
I am not the happy idiot

who speaks to the moon, that blind eye,
as the fawning subject speaks to his king
nor as the beggar whispers to his dog
when he hears the steps of cold death approaching.
I am not the carefree idiot
who sings his idiot song
to stars who know not how to sleep.
No. I have a path.
I am not here
to ring the silver bells of the fool's collar
before this sky of terrific immensity,
because the sky is not my master,
because the sky is not the haughty emperor of my destiny.
No.
I take no orders from the sky.
I am the one who watches over the sky.
The relentless spy
of this magical geometry of fearful stars,
of planets that turn
in accordance with exact laws.
I follow a path,
and that is my secret.

He hears the sound of steps.

What is that noise?
Who desecrates this bottomless darkness?
Someone is coming.

He hides. Enter Damascón.

damascón

Inconstant moon that arouses the assassin's instinct.
Capricious moon that separates or unites lovers on a whim.
Moon that strokes the loin of the sleeping dragon
to rumble his soul,
the clear fire of his soul.
Moon to which I owe the darkness of my thoughts,
the darkness of my origins
and the darkness of my destiny,
let us settle this debt.

He unsheathes his sword and points it at the moon.

God damn it.
This pilgrimage is making me maniacal.

He replaces the sword.

Along my journey I have lost my entourage.
My servants grew ill,
some died of snake bites, of fatigue,
of fevers that revealed to them the horrific face of delirium,
some deserted with the stealthy steps of reptiles,
taking with them the finest beasts,
the most noble horses,
chests of provisions…
To the devil with them.
Others stayed on in the villages we passed through,
eager to start new lives there as shrewd tradespeople;
others fled with ruined women,

others begged me, in tears, to let them return
to their families, and they kissed my feet,
and I despised them,
and I sent them to tie their necks by the limbs of rotten trees
so that they would cast not even a shadow.
And so it went until at last I was alone.
And now I wander abandoned lands,
the forbidden gardens of my enemies,
these dry fields.
I, King Damascón,
who has felt the metal of the sword
scrape against the metal of armor,
pierce the flesh
and chip the bone.
I, King Damascón,
who has heard the feet of death
splash about in the springs of blood,
when the battleground became a red whirlpool.
I, King Damascón,
who in one hamlet ordered 78 men beheaded
simply because I could,
if only to propagate my atrocious reputation,
to gain respect.
I, Damascón, of the light conscience,
friend of fast blood,
king who each night dreams
of heads rolling down the sides of mountains
and king who each morning made such heads roll
off the necks of poor devils who treasured their lives.

I, Damascón, the feared,
to find myself here, without food nor shelter,
in the harsh lands of strangers,
more than a year's journey away from my kingdom,
more than a century away from myself,
a ghost of myself,
following an uncertain star.

God damn it.

damascón

Who goes there?
What unfriendly nocturnal beast,
what gloomy songbird,
what pilgrim?
Who dares
cross my path,
to ululate in my night?
Who dares?

amerín *(emerging)*

Who suggests, traveler,
that this path is your path,
that this night is your night?
Who suggests, adventurer,
that it isn't indeed you

who disturbs my rest,
who invades my journey,
who causes my night to quiver?

damascón

Who are you?

amerín

Oh, let's just say there are many possibilities.
Let's just say I could be anyone
except you.
I could be a humble date-robber
or a greedy carpet-vendor.
I could be a murderer
or I could be the begrudging ghost of the murdered.
I could be the astute lover of all your women
or the frightened nomad who lost his compass
in a reckless bet.
I could be your king
or I could be the loose-tongued conspirer
imprisoned for slandering a petty king.

damascón

Quiet already.
Grate my ears no longer
with your meowing speech, you puppeteer.
Have you got anything to eat?

amerín

>   To eat?
>   What would you like, sir:
>   duck breast
>   with a jug of Greek wine
>   and a crusty knob of bread?

damascón

>   Are you laughing at me, you fool?

amerín

>   I would, if I were a fool, have no doubt of it.

damascón

>   Well if you are not a fool,
>   answer my question:
>   have you got anything to eat, fool?

amerín

>   Well … it depends on how you look at it.
>   When the moon casts its reflection
>   on that limestone,
>   I can assure you that it looks like a bowl of frothy milk
>   and you need only imagine
>   you are drinking it, and your thirst is satisfied.
>   If you make a bonfire
>   and singe a sprig of thyme in it,

I assure you that you shan't need a lamb
to imagine you are roasting a lamb.
And so on and so on.
Of illusory foods
you shall have plenty here, you may be sure of that.
So you may eat whatever you like.

damascón

That is just what I'll do.
But allow me to ask you another question…

amerín

My body is an eardrum.
Ask away, Mr. Inquisitive.

damascón

Yes, let's see.
What is the difference between stoning a toad
and tearing in two the head
of a ridiculous charlatan character
with whom you cross paths one night
in a wasteland?

amerín

Well, then, let's see…
Let me think on it a minute…
Because it is a great dilemma you have posed.

It would take at least 7 wise Babylonian men to solve it.
Let's see.
What is the difference between stoning a toad
and tearing in two the head
of a ridiculous charlatan character
with whom you cross paths one night
in a wasteland?
Hmmmm…
I'll try my luck: none?
There is no difference at all, is there?
Am I right, Mr. Inquisitive?

damascón

Yes, and now you shall receive a prize
for your great wisdom…

*He unsheathes his sword and attacks Amerín, who springs up,
leaps behind some element on the set and immediately emerges
with a large wooden sword.*

damascón

What a surprise.
Are you a brave fool?
Are you the comedian who wears a warrior disguise
with a sword made of timber?

amerín

No, Mr. Inquisitive.
I am King Amerín,
the happiest of all the kings of the East.
The king who scratches his back with his scepter.
The king who dies of laughter just looking at his feet.
He who governs from atop the golden armrest of his throne.
He who kills with a smile on his face.
So drop your vain sword
and put yourself at my service at once.

damascón

What an honor.   *(he bows)*
King Amerín,
famous for losing all battles,
celebrated for wearing the crown
with the same dignity
with which madmen wear
tricolor caps with bells.
King Amerín   *(another bow)*
whose legend spreads
throughout the land's most remote regions,
though that legend be
one of misery and cowardice,
of foolishness and weakness.
Though that legend
render you a fool
who plays with his kingdom

as children play
with captured birds.

amerín

The legend satisfies me,
for what is life after all
if not a game
in which everything is lost in advance
even though capricious Fortune
may align herself with us
and grant us the illusion that we are winning?
But who are you,
arrogant Mr. Inquisitive,
traveler of the quick sword?

damascón

I am King Damascón,
but have no fear.

amerín *(bowing)*

King Damascón,
the famous murderer with a crown,
the haughty king whom Lady Death
thanks every morning
for doing her work for her.
What an honor.   *(another bow)*

damascón *(defiant)*

Two kings are too many
for a kingdom as small
as this kingdom in the middle of nowhere,
this kingdom made of nothing,
this nothing in the midst of nothing,
made into the kingdom of nothing.

amerín *(derisive)*

The nothing of the nowhere of nothing
in the midst of the kingdom of nothing.
If we look at it that way,
I have no trouble whatsoever in bequeathing you
the portion of the nothing that may correspond to me
in this nothing of nowhere of nothing
in the middle of nowhere
in the kingdom of nothing.
This kingdom is yours, Damascón.

Amerín leaves, followed by Damascón.

King Kagba emerges, stealthily.

kagba

What a curious meeting
chance has contrived:
King Damascón and King Amerín,
the burning sun and the pale and frigid moon;
King Damascón and King Amerín:
the murmur of water that flows nowhere
and the whistle of boastful fire
that displaces its stature at every instant
because it would rather devour the universe.
And, in case they needed someone else,
chance has brought me here as well.
But who am I?
Well I am King Kagba,
the monarch they call fearful
for not believing in reasons of blood
for not sending his serfs to their deaths
for motives
that are often not worth
even the saliva it takes to formulate them.
Oh!
I did not ask for a kingdom,
but I inherited a kingdom.
I never once wanted a throne,
but since I was a child I have sat on a throne.
All my life
I have had to speak
with men kneeled down before me,

and I have barely seen a set of eyes.
I have always felt my power
like a dragon who rumbles in my ear,
like a stone god
who whispers great empty words,
like an imperturbable sphinx
who speaks to me in a language
made solely of enigmas.

Always, since I was a child,
since my treacherous destiny
made me lord of a kingdom of intrigue and gloom,
I have dreamed of our world
as an immense glass structure
always about to shatter.
And, truly,
every day the world breaks a little,
because effectively it is made of glass,
and on that broken glass we hurt ourselves,
as we walk all of our lives
on broken glass.

In my dreams
the world is, I tell you,
a clean glass labyrinth,
an infinite extension of throbbing glass,
a transparent geometry.
Every night I have this dream,
and I suffer the anguish

of watching how
the earth we walk
breaks in brilliant fragments,
the snow-capped mountains,
the trees, slaves unto themselves,
the restless sea
that changes its monstrous face every second…

Everything breaks in my dreams.
Because in my dreams
the world is a glass sphere,
and it goes on breaking,
and it goes on leaving bits of glass,
and I step on the glass in my dreams,
and my feet bleed,
and I feel fear,
because everything is made of glass.

…But let us analyze the situation:
three wandering kings
in this no-man's-land,
in this nameless region.
A king with the happy spirit of a fool,
a king who has made himself death's friend
and a king — I — who has never known how to reign
and who has nothing in this world
but a golden crown.

What a strange confabulation of destinies:
the three of us lost here,
under a sky of stars in constant escape.
What a strange confabulation,
what a curious thing…

Something unknown to me warns me
that I am in danger,
because one is always in danger
in this world of glass.
I will pass for a beggar,
since the king
who abases himself to stain his sword
with the blood of a pauper
has yet to be born
and in that way
I may continue on my path unknown.

Enter Amerín, followed by Damascón, his sword raised.

kagba

Welcome the pilgrim.
Welcome, in the name of charity, the pilgrim
who goes this cold night without a path,
without a roof under which to sleep,
without a bed in which to tame his nightmares.

damascón

Who is this puppet?

amerín

Who is this skeletal ghost?

damascón

What are you doing here, sibylline phantom of night?

amerín (*mimicking him*)

What are you doing here, sibylline phantom of night?

kagba

Welcome to the pilgrim,
charity to the rambler,
compassion for the lost.

amerín

Do you also want something to eat,
pauper?
Smoked dragon meat,
brains of a three-headed eagle,
pointy ears of fallen angel?
Which do you fancy, pauper?
We have everything here.

kagba

Highest dignities,
illustrious wanderers,
lords of the desert,
I only ask
that you let me spend the night in your company,
because for three days I have been plagued by pests
I have never seen,
and which lie in wait for me, invisible,
and I hear their muffled roar in the darkness,
and I know they are waiting for a moment of weakness
to devour me.

damascón

One sees in this plateau
even beasts go hungry.
Tell us your name, pauper.

kagba

Kagba is my name, my lord,
and I assure you that you can trust in my character,
and that if you were to squeeze my heart,
not one drop of poison would fall.

damascón

You hold yourself in high esteem, pauper,
because there is no human heart that can presume
  innocence.

All hearts are dark labyrinths,
and in all hearts a spider
weaves prisons to keep our destiny captive.

amerín (*mocking*)

Dark as a labyrinth in the dark.
Sinister as a sinister cave.
Throbbing as a beating organ.
That is how the heart is, pauper.

damascón (*to Amerín*)

Shall we tear open his breast to contemplate
his immaculate heart?

amerín (*to Damascón*)

Let us.
I have always liked to play with hearts.

kagba (*to Damascón*)

Lord, be merciful.
Think of my heart as the scrap that despises the hyena.
Proclaim to the four winds
that my heart is the rotten fruit
that hangs from the scorched tree.
But leave it, I beg you, in its place.

damascón *(laughing)*

> I see you hold your heart in high esteem, pauper.
> I advise you to keep it pure as long as you can,
> for there is no muscle more fragile nor more fickle.

kagba

> I shall do so, my lord,
> and you, recall the legend that says
> he who pardons the life of a pauper
> gains one hundred hours of sleep in paradise.

damascón

> If you could see the paradise of which I dream each night,
> I assure you you would have an eternal vision of hell.

amerín

> Damascón's paradise
> is a sea of blood, pauper.
> A place in which archangels swirl about,
> their heads cut open,
> like birds without eyes.

kagba

> Well that is a strange paradise…
> Headless archangels,
> their wings stained with blood…
> very strange indeed.

damascón

> I am beginning to grow tired of you two.
> I need to rest,
> because my journey is long,
> so silence, please.

amerín

> What journey is not long, Damascón?
> What journey has an end?

kagba

> There are infinite journeys…

damascón

> I said silence, loudmouths!

amerín

> Yes, Damascón, silence in the blind night,
> because the night is blind,
> and the moon is the eye of the blind night…
> Go into the darkness, Damascón.
> Close your eyes and sleep.
> And devour, in your dream, a reptile's entrails.

kagba

Yes, devour, in your dream, a reptile's entrails,
Damascón.

amerín

Psssst, because the night is blind…
Psssst…

[end of act one]

Act Two

The three kings continued on their pilgrimage in unison, wandering nameless regions, vigilant and starving, yearning for celebrations and battles, sentries even of their shadows, and in this way they had occasion to establish a bizarre complicity founded in mutual distrust, as each one kept it a secret unto himself the true motive behind his disheartened journey, not knowing that their motives were one and the same, as all three were following the same star, and no longer even suspecting the reason behind that enigmatic pursuit, as well as the essence of the unreasonableness that incited them to wander remote regions of the land in the mode of vagabonds, abandoning their respective kingdoms to the blows of chance magic and to the whims of scheming stewards.

Kagba, Amerín, and Damascón, the three monarchs exiled by the influence of one bewitched star, talked continuously to one another, as that was their way of fighting one another.

amerín *(to Damascón)*

And I'll tell you what else, vain king,
king of bloodied moons,
lord of killer metals,
I'll tell you what:
when you return to your kingdom,
if you do indeed return,
rest assured that no one will have wept for your absence,
rest assured that your serfs
will have been happy without you,
knowing that their heads would not roll down the
    gallows
like vanishing masks,
on the whim of their king,
the horrific king Damascón,
who cleans the blood off the blade of his sword
with more blood;
rest assured
that those generals, priests, and ministers
who kissed your feet
will have now sat at the throne of another tyrant,
surely one as despicable as yourself,
because they need a grotesque and arrogant leader
in whose shadow they may seek refuge
and maintain their power
in their miserable way,
as fever maintains power in the ill.

damascón *(laughing)*

Yes, Amerín,
vain king of a vain crown,
monarch of puppet theater,
happy sovereign of farce,
yes,
it is possible that my people only remember me now
as one remembers in the morning
the nocturnal fall to the abyss,
as the troubled sleeper remembers
the mouth of the dragon who devours him
every time he shuts his eyes
and gives in
to the deformations of sleep.
I do not refute it.
And you, in contrast,
I am sure your serfs cry for you every day,
I am sure that they throw themselves desperately
off the royal towers
because they long for the talent of your majesty,
your good sense,
your value on the battefield.
I am sure that they despise life
because they miss your magnificent marionette,
the smiling dummy
that pranced around
atop a golden carriage,
the regal toad that jumped over the moon

reflected in puddles.
Yes, Amerín,
I am sure that when you return to your kingdom,
if death does not
stroke your empty head first,
your people will receive you
with the ringing of oboes and kettledrums,
with torches of jubilation,
with sacrifices, with moving hymns.
I am sure that your people will cry with happiness,
like a single giant eye,
before the return of the triumphant warrior,
before the glorious homecoming of the prophet of
    radiant foolishness.
I am sure of it, Amerín.

kagba

Is a kingdom without its king
less bad than a king without his kingdom?

damascón

Are you a pauper or a philosopher?
What do you know of kingdoms and kings?
What do you know about what it is to feel
the claw of power itself in the chest,
that claw that tries to rip your heart out by its roots
so that nothing can hide there,
so that no weak feeling

may make the heart its chamber?
What do you know?

kagba

What I hear here and there,
my lord,
what they tell me,
the legends that spread
throughout every kingdom in the land,
because you both are the kings of legend,
objects of gossip and speculation,
incentives for fable and fantasy,
and a vagabond such as myself has never
had occasion to appreciate from so close up
the grandness of the soul not only of a king,
which in and of itself would dazzle anybody,
but that of two monarchs of such great understanding.

damascón

Such great understanding?
Such great understanding
that we are here,
not knowing where to go,
not knowing where we are,
and unable to even imagine
where we will be tomorrow?

amerín

Such great understanding,
such great understanding
that my feet ask me each night:
"Where will you take us at sunrise,
my lord?"
And I answer them: "If you two don't know,
who could tell you?"
Not even my feet
know where they step,
and they are growing rebellious,
and conspire against me,
and I do not have them locked up in a dungeon
for a very simple reason:
because they are my feet.

kagba

Well then return, my majesties, to your kingdoms.
What prevents you?

damascón

That's what I'd like to know…
What prevents me
from retracing my steps,
abandoning this foolish adventure,
returning to my land,
placing myself before my troops,

and demolishing any neighboring region
so that the world forgets me not,
so that the world knows
that each day it has cause to tremble?
Because I have been
the shadow of death upon the world.

amerín *(joking, aside)*

Uhh, the shadow of death upon the world…
The world of death among the shadow…
The death of the shadow upon the world…

damascón *(to Kagba)*

Well… You, pauper,
find some well over there
and bring me some water.
And look to see if there is any animal to eat,
repugnant though it may be.
I shall go myself to hunt it,
be it a beast of seven heads.

kagba

You may count on it, King Damascón.
I shall be vigilant,
for if I make out any creature
hidden in the entrails of the earth,
any mythical bird,

be it half-crow half-vulture,
be it the oldest witch in the land;
a newt emerged from a swamp,
a dribbling monster
dragging itself like a snake
roaring the roar of a lion.
Consider it done.

He exits.

amerín

Do you think the pauper
capable of finding
not the most frightful beast in the East,
but even a well that is not as dry
as our hearts?

damascón

No, I do not think him so,
but at least he will be out of sight
for a while.
There is something cheerless
in that pauper.
The elusive shadow of he who lies.

amerín

Well, Damascón,
if you do not trust in the hunting capacities

of that globe-trotting ghost,
let us go ourselves and hunt.
Let us recall the times of glory,
when our dogs barked before daybreak
because they smelled already the blood of wild beasts.
Let us go, Damascón,
let us kill at least the visible,
and return with the corpse of wind as our trophy.

damascón

Yes, Amerín,
let us go play at killing.

amerín

Let us play.

They exit. Kagba enters, stealthily.

kagba

The night is too deep.
Not even the haughty moon
can lighten so much blackness today.
It seems the stars are dead
and I step in this fine sand
as one steps into the depths of a sea.
What a disturbing adventure,
what blinded wandering.
In my journey Lucifer passed me.

Three times, under different disguises.
And three times he tempted me,
and three times I managed to escape him,
despite that his words
seduced me,
because Lucifer speaks
the sweet language of charmers.
That evil showed itself to me
under the guise of a wizard,
and warned me that in my kingdom,
during my absence,
the greed of the tradesmen,
the ambition of the stewards,
the triumph of swine
had all come undone…
All was chaos there,
he told me, and the streams of blood capricious.
"Return to your kingdom," Lucifer told me.
"Return immediately to your kingdom,
save it, King Kagba,
that your portion of the world
not be one more region of hell."
But I covered my ears and continued on my way.
The second time,
Lucifer approached me disguised as a doctor.
"Are you King Kagba?" he asked me.
"Well, I come from your land, fugitive king.
And I must tell you that the people there are dying
like leaves in autumn,

consumed by an epidemic brought from Cathay
by spice traders.
The dying weep in the absence of their king,
they yearn for the protection of their monarch,
and they wonder: Why will our lord not save us?"
But I covered my ears once again.
The third time,
the devil approached me
in the form of a sibyl,
and was a beautiful woman with dark eyes,
and her voice was soft,
as the intimate whisper of death must be,
and told me that my journey
would lead to nothing itself,
that my pilgrimage would be fruitless,
that the star I follow
is only an errant imagination of the night,
and invited me to lie with her,
to rejoice in her supple body,
to forget the world in her arms,
to quiet my words in her mouth.
But I paid her no heed and I carried on,
and here I find myself,
searching for beasts that may be devoured
by three hungry kings,
while up above
the mysterious star
speaks to me in a language I do not understand.

He exits.

*Enter Damascón and Amerín. They begin hunting an
imaginary animal, and end up fighting one another,
until a blinding light invades the stage.*

damascón

What light dares in the night?
What insolent light
comes to deny the night?
What shines in this murdered night?

amerín

It is the haughty time of the star.
It is the shimmering voice of the star.
The time has come to listen to it.

damascón

Close your eyes, Amerín.
This light is mine alone.

amerín

Close your eyes, Damascón,
because this light shines for me.

[end of act two]

Act Three

Was it a catastrophe of light? Was it the excruciating glare of the end of a world or the sign of the prodigious birth of a world? Was it the sumptuous death of a star or the radiant manifestation of an ignored and haughty god in need of adoration?

Whatever it was, the three lost kings continued their colloquium, and the volatile substance of the hallucination swept the night like a foolish ghost, and the crowned puppets turned about themselves, as if the universe had the dimensions of a shadow puppet theater.

kagba

Look at a golden crown
in the light of the moon
and it will seem a trinket.
Look at a silver necklace
in the plain light of day
and its poverty will shock you.
The sun is the enemy of gold
and the moon is the sister of silver.
In the same way,
thought shines in darkness,
radiant thought seeks refuge
in gloom,
and wavers before brightness,
because it is light before light,
while insanity,
because it is full of shadow,
grows with the sun,
and you will see the insane
exhibit his madness gleefully
in markets and plazas,
prancing about, screaming,
braiding his visionary speech,
bathed in brightness,
just as the wise man
awaits the moon
to withdraw into himself,
to decipher in the stars

the luminous calligraphy of his god,
to read in the blackness of the sky
the enigmas
answered by other enigmas.

Enter Damascón.

damascón

Talking to your shadow, pauper?

kagba

I am talking to King Kagba.

damascón

King Kagba?

kagba

I am talking to myself, Damascón.
I am talking to King Kagba.

damascón *(laughing)*

You, a king?
Have you lost all reason?
Have you dreamed the dream of power
and continued to daydream of it?

kagba

> I am King Kagba.
> I am the true dream of a king.
> I am the king
> who has never awoken from that dream.

> *Enter Amerín.*

amerín

> Who speaks of dreaming?
> It has been three nights already
> I have not shut my eyes.
> Three nights already
> that my vigil turns the hours I deny sleep
> into nightmares.

damascón

> The pauper has gone mad.
> Now he says he is a king.

amerín

> He must not have slept, either…
> Or he has slept too much.
> Are you a king, pauper?
> Well then, praise be to the monarch!
> Because we must bear in mind
> that, on occasion,

dreams invert destinies, is it not so?
You daydream that you are a pauper
and, when you achieve sleep, you dream you are a king.
You are a king who lives his haughty dream of being a king
and, as soon as you close your eyes,
you dream that you beg in the poor quarters of your
    kingdom,
and that dogs bark at you,
and that your subjects throw stones at you.
A dream is the fiction of another fiction,
a snake that swallows itself.
The pauper must be talking in his sleep.

kagba

I am King Kagba.
I am the monarch of a kingdom
in which everyone trembles
because there, the future
is only a bad premonition,
a fearful foreboding in the plain light of day,
an anguish that grows by night.
I am King Kagba,
sovereign of a land of glass.

damascón

King Kagba?
The king of that kingdom so small
that it has never been invaded

because no other king can be bothered
to take up the work
of ordering it conquered?

amerín

The king of that kingdom so miniscule
that it could be squashed
by the clumsy foot of a carnival giant?

kagba

I am King Kagba.

damascón

Well, when I return to my kingdom,
I will order yours destroyed, pauper king.
I will order it burned
from one end to the other
so that you are the monarch of a kingdom of smoke.

amerín

With your crown of smoke.

kagba

Burn my kingdom?
Well, I'll tell you, haughty Damascón,
that that way the birds will see it from atop their perches
as the most beautiful of all the kingdoms of the land,

because the embers will make it seem
an immensity of amber.

damascón

No, not an immensity of amber.
A simple kingdom in flames, pauper king.
One of the thousands of kingdoms that have burned
before your time
and one of the thousands that shall burn
after you are dead.

kàgba

Yes, Damascón.
Many kingdoms shall burn
after both you and I are dead.
Many.
But I will avoid the suffering of seeing them burn,
while you will endure the dissatisfaction
of not seeing the land wrapped in flames.

damascón

What do you know, beggar king?
What do you know of the pact I have made
with that god of light
who has come to visit me
in this infinite desert?

kagba

A god of light?
A god who has come to visit you?
And who has perhaps offered you immortality,
the unending dream of power,
the eternal nightmare of the delirious?
Have you promised that god
that you will watch as the planets,
the suns, the uncertain stars, consume themselves,
as the sea evaporates,
as the sky falls heavily above the sterile land,
and that you will stay young and always haughty,
sending your soldiers off to their deaths?
No.
What you have seen, naïve Damascón,
is but a mirage of divinity,
the visionary shape
of a god who can have no shape,
because he is made of himself,
and his substance is invisible.

amerín

A god without shape?
An invisible substance?
I think I am lost,
lofty majesties,
and humbly I bow
before your abstract wisdom.

But I ask myself,
and it is only a question, of course,
a question asked by a king
who has gone three nights sleepless,
is it possible that we are
like those silly moths that flutter around senselessly
around an open fire,
bewitched,
until they burn in the flames?

damascón

For years I have watched
the movements of that star
that I saw die three nights ago.
For years
I have dreamed of deciphering
its radiant mystery,
its enigmatic message,
and now that mystery is mine,
and now I am the owner of that enigma.

amerín

Enigma, Damascón?
The enigma
of the suicide of light?

kagba

> What enigma has an owner, Damascón?
> He who owns an enigma
> is never its proprietor,
> but rather its victim.
> But… Do you hear the sea?

damascón

> The sea?
> Are you delirious, pauper?

amerín

> What sea do you hear,
> king of a scepter of smoke?
> A sea as deep as insanity,
> a sea of fish seeking the horizon,
> a sea atop whose surface float
> all the corpses of conscience?
> What sea do you hear?

kagba

> I hear the trembling of a ghost of water.

damascón

> God damn you to hell,
> pauper king of the paupers,
> how can you hear the sea in this empty desert

in which one hears only the crunch
of breaking stars?

kagba

    I see the invisible.
    I hear the nonexistent.
    I think what cannot be imagined.
    I even imagine
    what the imagination cannot imagine.

amerín

    Our beggar king
    must be a wizard.
    I cannot even manage to see what I see.
    I cannot even hear the sound of my memory.
    My thought is a phantom
    that flees from itself.
    I cannot even imagine what I could imagine.

damascón

    Well I can imagine.
    I can imagine the metallic murmur of an army
    advancing in secret on the enemy front.
    I can imagine
    the roar of thousands of throats
    swollen with pride and with panic.
    I can imagine

the haughty blood that stains a vanquished land.
I can imagine a world that kneels
before the passing of a golden carriage.

kagba

A golden carriage
in which you, supposedly, travel,
Damascón, the undefeated.
A golden carriage
pulled by dragons
that roar frightened
by the thunder of the crowd that applauds you.

damascón

Are you asking me to behead you, pauper?

kagba

No one asks for such a thing as that,
you may be sure of it.
Even the criminal most terrified of himself
whines and begs clemency
when he walks in broken steps to the gallows.
But you can assassinate me whenever you wish,
Damascón.
Nothing is stopping you.
No one could stop you,
much less your rotten soul.

damascón

Do not abuse your luck nor my patience,
petty king.

amerín

You heard him, Kagba:
do not abuse Damascón's infinite patience.
Do not put his goodness to the test.
Do not approach the edge of his sword.

damascón

You neither,
happy Amerín.
Terror on the faces of fools amuses me greatly.

amerín

No, no, Damascón.
It is not worth killing me.
I have been sleepless three nights.
Three nights.
Three nights without closing these eyes
that look without seeing.
That is the same as being dead,
floating in who knows what horrific eternity,
together with other winged corpses.
It is better to kill this one.

damascón

God damn you both…
Be quiet for once, marionettes.
I am returning to my kingdom.
You may perish here.

amerín

Farewell, Damascón.
May the magic star bring you along a good path.
May snakes coil themselves around your neck as you sleep.
May the water of the fountains taste to you like poison.
May the poison they put in your cup taste like syrup.
May death visit you with the slowness of gangrene.

damascón (exiting)

I wish the same upon you.

kagba (to amerín)

What will you do?

amerín

Me? Easy: I will sleep.
I will dream I am following a star.
I will dream I am the owner of a star.
I will dream that I am traveling in that star

just like in a shooting star.
And then I will wake up. And we shall see.

Amerín falls asleep.

kagba

Sleep, imprudent Amerín.
Dream of that star
that has led us to this delirium.
But where shall I go?
What shall I tell those who ask me?
What logic will this nightmare hold?
I do not know where to go.
I do not know.

And the night is blind.

And I shall never come out of the night.

And I shall never come out of the night.

[the end]

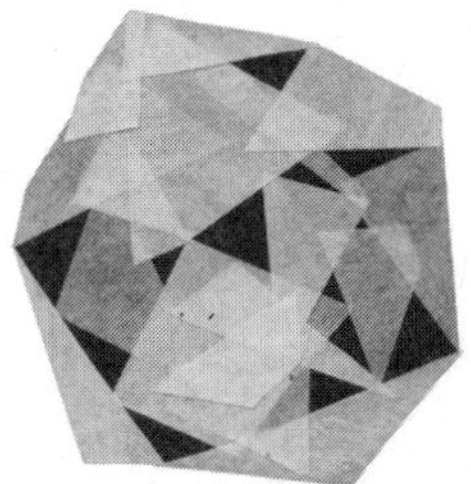

Felipe Benítez Reyes

was born in Cádiz, in 1960. Among his literary distinctions are the Luis Cernuda Prize, the Nadal Prize, the National Book Award, and the National Critics Award for his 1996 collection *Vidas improbables* (of which an English translation was published by BOA Editions in 2006). He lives in the town of Rota, Andalusia, with his wife, the translator Silvia Barbero.

Emily Toder

was born in New York City, in 1981. She has translated the poetry and prose of Edgar Bayley, Laura Campmany, Luis Chaves, and Laura Fernández, among others. Her first poetry collection, *Science*, was published in 2012 by Coconut Books.